Teach me right

Jade I'Anson-Milner

Copyright © 2023 Jade I'Anson-Milner

All rights reserved.

Published by Andrew Milner Books

ISBN: 978-1-7384110-0-9

For my dad, the man who taught me right.
I hope I am making you proud.

Contents

Chapter 1: The Brain

Chapter 2: Memory and Learning

Chapter 3: Critical periods

Chapter 4: The difference between the adult and adolescent brain

Chapter 5: Teenage behaviour

Chapter 6: Can adolescents learn?

Chapter 7: History of teaching teenagers

Chapter 8: Importance of student-led teaching

Chapter 9: What does teaching teenagers look like?

Chapter 10: Poverty and the adolescent brain

Chapter 11: Socialisation

Chapter 12: Technology

Chapter 13: Fast-paced environment

Chapter 14: Real-life experiences

Chapter 15: Think Four Approach

Chapter 16: Best outcomes for learners

Acknowledgments

A special thank you to Jo Tejo and the amazing Institute of Health and Life Sciences team I get to call colleagues.
A special thank you to Su Tovey for putting up with my thousand questions each week.
Thank you to Kelly Ackroyd for sparking my love of neuroscience.

Preface

The Education and Skills Act (2008) made education compulsory until the age of 18 by 2015, with the premise for this legislative change being to improve employability, upskill young people and increase participation in higher education. In 2021, only 81.2% of 16–18-year-olds were engaged in compulsory education, with 5% of 16–18-year-olds not in education, employment or training. Of the 81.2 percent, on average, only 84% of students achieved their qualification. The increase in those not in education, employment, or training (NEETS) is particularly alarming when we consider a large percentage of these students start college or sixth form at 16 before dropping out of formal education. These statistics pose two questions, why are adolescents dropping out of education? And why are those in education not all achieving?

There are of course many factors to consider, including socio-economics, special educational needs and disabilities and poverty. While all these factors do indeed require consideration, we must also consider the specific neurological events taking place within the adolescent brain and scrutinise our own teaching practices to examine their effectiveness in meeting these neurological needs.

In 2019, the complex nature of the adolescent brain formed the basis of my MA in Education. My research allowed me to explore the way the adolescent brain learns whilst simultaneously adapting teaching strategies to better suit these unique needs. This book is based upon those findings and the teaching strategies found to better support the adolescent brain in learning.

1: The Brain

Before we dive into the nitty, gritty of the workings of the adolescent brain, we must first explore the science behind the make-up of the brain. Afterall, we cannot hope to understand how the brain learns if we don't first have an understanding of what the brain is. Obviously, I am an educator and not a scientist, neuroscientist, neurologist or any type of expert relating to brain design or the complexities within it, so when I say this chapter is a brief introduction into the make-up of the brain, that is exactly what I mean.

The brain is the most complex organ in the human body. It is the home of intelligence, the controller of emotions and behaviour and initiator of body movement and function. In a bony shell, the brain is the source of all the qualities that define humanity.

The brain is comprised of four complex specialised areas that work together. These specialised areas are the cortex, the brain stem, the basal ganglia and the cerebellum. The cortex is the outer most layer of the brain. Thinking and voluntary movements begin in the cortex. The brain stem sits between the spinal cord and the rest of the brain, controlling basic essential functions like breathing and sleeping. The basal ganglia are a cluster of structures in the centre of the brain. The basal ganglia is responsible for coordinating messages between multiple other brain areas. The cerebellum sits at the base of the brain, taking control of balance and coordination (Hestenes 1987)

The brain is also made up of several lobes. Frontal, parietal, temporal and occipital. Each of these lobes takes responsibility for physical, emotional and intellectual functions. The frontal lobe takes responsibility for problem solving and judgement and motor functions. The parietal lobes manage sensation, handwriting and body position. The temporal lobes are involved in memory and hearing. The occipital lobes contain the brain's visual processing system. It is important to remember that while the different lobes and cortexes take a significant amount of responsibility for specific functions, the implementation of those functions is not completely dependent on that one lobe or cortex alone. Throughout the process of brain development, different cortexes and lobes take on more prominent roles. This is in part due to hormonal changes and experiences (we will explore this in greater detail later in this book). Neuroplasticity also plays an important role in this. Indeed, it is important to remember neuroplasticity and its role in the developing brain. Neuroplasticity can be described as an umbrella term used to describe the brain's ability to adapt and change both structurally and functionally throughout life in response to experiences. Indeed, the brain is malleable (Bene and Dermarin 2014) When we say the brain is malleable that doesn't mean it is like a ball of playdough that can be rolled, squished and pulled apart, it simply means different cortexes and lobes can become bigger or reduce in size due to experiences or in some cases, lack of experiences. The process of neuroplasticity also allows the brain to rewire itself after the brain experiences an accident or trauma that damages a part of the brain to ensure important functions are not lost.

2: Memory and learning

Memory and learning are two separate entities and while they work together, they do not equate to the same thing. There are two different types of memory, short term and long term. Just as its name suggests, short term memory allows us to recall information for a short period of time such as remembering a number until we can write it down or remembering facts until we have passed a test. Remembering a fact or a number until we can write it down does not mean we have learnt those facts or that number. I can clearly remember spending hours reading and rereading flashcards, each containing a historical fact I would need to remember to pass my history exam. Those hours spent repeating facts paid off and I passed the exam but a week later I could not remember half of the facts I had so carefully memorised.

Learning requires desire, self-belief, and willingness. Learning is not something that can be done to another person. As teachers we do not have the power to force our students to learn. We can quiz them, test them, talk at them, and question them but we cannot make them learn. We may think we have accomplished learning when our students pass a test, indeed schools and colleges are graded on the achievement percentages of exams such as G.C.S.E and A levels. Passing a test does not equate to real learning.

The brain is a busy organ. Probably the busiest in the body. To be as effective as it possibly can be it must be efficient. Efficiency means pruning information not deemed essential or important. Our brains are constantly absorbing information, taking in the things we see and hear, the things we are told (Pastor 2020) Our brains receive and process so much information that a lack of efficiency would result in a brain overload. To avoid this the clever organ that is the brain prunes away the information it deems to be unnecessary. It often makes these decisions without conscious effort or thought; yes, you read that right. Our brain decides what information we need to keep and what information it can get rid of simply through the way the information is presented. When we teach to the test, and tell learners that this is the information they need to pass that exam, this is the information they need to remember for the exam, their brain views this as, I just need to remember this until the exam and so, just like my history exam many years ago, once the exam is over the brain, in its efficiency, prunes away that information believing it is no longer needed. It does that because as teachers we have unwittingly told it to through the way we have presented the information to them, through the words we have said and the learning environment we have created. What a scary thought that is, because as teachers, our purpose is to help our learners gain the knowledge and skills required to be successful, self-sufficient individuals and yet our approach to teaching results in the absolute opposite taking place. Learners are being spoon-fed the information required to pass those all-important exams, removing any need for self-sufficiency, instead making these learners dependent upon those individuals who are supposed to be preparing them for life.

There has been an argument made in previous years that the

reason learners forget information upon completion of an exam is that schools and educational institutions provide them with cognitive overload (Chandler and Sweller 1991) We simply expect learners to remember too much, suggesting, just like memory sticks and hard-drives, our memories have a capacity. Thankfully, this is not true. While our short-term memory only holds information for a short time, our long-term memory has a limitless capacity. Anything our brain deems important enough to remember is stored in our long-term memory. Due to its limitless capacity the brain files memories away from the forefront of our minds and brings them back to the forefront when they are needed through the process of memory retrieval. If then memory has a limitless capacity, why is the information presented in class not making it into storage, why can it not be recalled once the exam is over through the process of memory retrieval? The answer is simple. We are not presenting the information to them in a way that stimulates long-term memory processes. We are more likely to remember information when it is something we understand, are interested in, were engaged in learning, or have linked the information to an emotion. Smells are a common trigger for memory retrieval. The smell of fresh grass or a perfume can take us back to childhood games on the playing field or our grandma's house at Christmas. This is because our brain has made a connection between the smell and a memory. In the same way a specific emotion can bring back memories. Often memories linked to emotion are negative ones, with many sufferers from PTSD finding memories triggered by emotions to be traumatic (Ehlers, Hackmann and Michael 2004) Memories triggered by smells, sounds and emotions are often spontaneous memories, memories that are brought to our subconscious for no specific purpose at the time. Enjoyment can also be a trigger for memory retrieval. When we have experienced something enjoyable our brains naturally want to keep hold of that memory in the hope of recreating that feeling of enjoyment again. Indeed, we actively want to remember experiences of joy and happiness. We want to be able to recall these frequently, to make ourselves feel better or to share the story with others. Think about Christmas dinner or a family gathering, people often share stories from years past, reliving memories of happy times spent together or with those that are no longer here. If then, happy emotions can support memory retention and recall, should we not be creating a learning environment that fosters feelings of enjoyment and happiness?

We have a huge responsibility as tutors and teachers of adolescent learners to prepare them for a happy and prosperous future. Many think this responsibility begins and ends with a test, a grade and a qualification. This could not be further from the truth.

3: Critical Periods – truth or myth

While the brain is constantly developing and changing, there are times when the brain is developing more rapidly, with some of the most important synapse and neural connections forming during this time. These periods of time are called critical periods (Gale et al 2003)

The most well-known critical period within development is that which takes place during the early years. Indeed, during the first five years of life the brain goes through intensive development, with some of the most important and critical connections being formed. These connections are interlinked with all areas of development. The neurons required for the most essential physical development.

Babies are born with all the brain cells they will ever need; however, it is the connections between these cells that are the most important. These connections enable us to move, communicate, think and do just about everything else. The early years are without doubt crucial in building and developing these connections. These connections are referred to as synapses. In the early years at least one million new neural connections are made each second, more than any other time in life. Due to this, the early years are viewed as being the most essential years in development. Whilst the early years are indeed critical, they are not the only years that provide a platform for crucial development to take place, the period of adolescence is equally as important. During adolescence an important reorganisation of the brain occurs which allows for essential psychological and emotional development to occur at a much deeper level (Casey, Jones and Somervile 2011) Indeed, just like the early years period, during adolescence the brain once again develops more neurons and synapses than needed (Blakemore and Choudhury 2006) During the period of adolescence, the brain once again undergoes a significant pruning process, this time however, there is less focus on overall development and more focus on the development of specific regions, lobes and cortexes within the brain. The key thing we need to remember here is that these skills are developing, not developed. During this critical period of brain development adolescents are trying to figure out who they are as a person as well as developing an understanding of the wider world and society. The desire adolescents have to do this is not a conscious decision on their part but rather is a product of neuroplasticity and the changes taking place in the brain during this critical period. The ability to think critically and to engage with abstract concepts is essential for real, effective and deep learning to take place. As educators we need to tailor our teaching in such a way that it supports this period of development. In a nutshell, the brain works its hardest during the periods of early years and adolescence, which may explain why teenagers seem to regress into the sleeping habits of a young child.

4: The difference between the adult and adolescent brain

The misconception that the brain is fully developed and therefore functioning in the same ways as an adult brain by the time adolescence is reached is one of the most significant contributing factors in the lack of understanding teachers have of adolescent learners. When we make the assumption that adolescent learners have the same control over their decision-making processes and behaviours as we as adults do, we run the risk of viewing a large percentage of our learners as being difficult, challenging or simply a lost cause when it comes to education. The reality is during adolescence the brain is only just starting to truly develop those critical thinking and decision-making abilities.

Another common misconception amongst adults and educational institutions is that adolescents are impulsive. They make snap decisions without considering the consequences which may occur later. Adolescents often put themselves in dangerous situations through their seeming impulsivity. In reality, the opposite of this is true. Rather than not thinking or being impulsive, the adolescent brain actually overthinks (Howard-Jones 2016) Research carried out through the use of MRI's shows that far from being impulsive the adolescent brain overthinks decisions and actions (Howard-Jones 2007) The adolescent brain's tendency to overthink decisions and actions comes as a result of the increased use of the limbic system. The way the limbic system controls emotions results in this overthinking, the limbic system and therefore their emotions, have become the driving force behind their thinking. The emotion of fear and of getting something wrong is a huge worry for teenagers despite the cool exterior they often present. If teenagers overthink, surely they should be the most cautious amongst us? If they overthink their decisions, choices and actions why do they still appear to be impulsive? Those working in education will undoubtedly have seen teenagers do something that we view as ridiculous and when asked why they did that the simple reply is usually, "I don't know," don't fall for that. They do know why they do things, it is just difficult for them to explain sometimes.

I am sure everybody has at some point in their lives rolled their eyes and explained teenage behaviour as hormones running wild or has actually been that teenager. Despite my teenage years being well and truly behind me I can still remember my dad rolling his eyes numerous times while blaming mine and my sister's behaviour on our raging hormones, particularly when one of us was crying over something that he perceived to be trivial. An eye roll, box of tissues and a tub of ice cream was the solution in my dad's eyes; that and a cuddle once we had stopped wailing uncontrollably. To some extent his, and many others, ideas that the dramatic, strange and often fast-paced adolescent behaviour was a result of out-of-control hormones is correct. Hormones have a significant influence on our behaviours, even in adulthood. Indeed, hormones are not a teenage phenomenon that disappear once we reach adulthood, our brains just simply learn to manage and regulate them more effectively as it matures.

The adolescent brain produces copious amounts of stress hormones, sex hormones and growth hormones, in greater measure than in both childhood and adulthood (Crone et al

2010) The increased amount of these hormones surging through the brain is partly to blame for the mood swings and erratic behaviour often displayed by teenagers. While both adults and teenagers experience hormones, the way the brain processes them is different. The adult brain processes hormones and hormonal reactions by engaging numerous cortexes and systems within the brain simultaneously. When hormones increase, due to stress, fear or other emotions the limbic system engages and reacts, creating feelings of anger or anxiety, producing the flight or fight reaction. At the same time the adult brain engages the prefrontal cortex, with this cortex playing a role in decision making, helping to keep negative urges and reactions in check. The adolescent brain, however, does not have the same level of simultaneous cortex and system engagement. During the adolescent period the limbic system is the most active and engaged area of the brain, with the limbic system often demonstrating over-stimulation and engagement. This increased use of the limbic system provides some explanation for the mood swings and erratic behaviour displayed by teenagers during the adolescent years (Steinberg 2008)

Not only does simultaneous engagement of different cortexes allow the adult brain to keep control of and regulate their emotions, it also allows deeper levels of thinking and analysing to occur. The adult brain is capable of considering the future and of setting future goals, be it academic, work related or personal. Buying a house is a good example of this. If you want to buy a house you need to do two things, the first thing is save a deposit and the second thing is to get a mortgage. While saving money is not something many people enjoy doing, the adult brain is capable of visualising the endpoint or the benefits and outcomes of staying away from the coffee shop each morning and saving that money for the deposit. The adolescent brain has not yet developed that level of forward thinking. The phrase money burns a hole in your pocket has never been more applicable than it has to teenagers. I have yet to meet a teenager who saves money willingly. As soon as most teenagers get money in their pocket they are going to spend it. Your local Primark will be packed on a weekend with teenagers wanting to spend their cash and those teenagers old enough to go out and party (and those that are not let's be honest) think nothing of spending £100 in one night. It may seem like this is impulsive behaviour but remember teenagers are actually less impulsive than adults. They are simply motivated by different rewards to adults. While as adults we can see the value of saving money and owning our own home in the future, teenagers are motivated by their emotions and their desire for peer-approval and acceptance. If having the latest clothes, the latest phone or drinking the most shots is viewed as peer-approved behaviour than it is well worth spending their cash on.

Emotions don't only motivate the spending habits of teenagers but also their enthusiasm for education and learning. Teenagers place friendships, relationships and socialisation in higher importance than education, attainment and future goals or accomplishments (Fenstein 2004) As children, teenagers and adults we have dreams and ideas of what we would like to be, what professions we would like to go into and what promotions or positions we would like to hold. When we are young some of these dreams and ideas can be a little bit out there. When I was younger, I was convinced I was going to be a princess when I grew up. As we get a little older, we bring our expectations more in line with reality, often choosing a profession that is more attainable than making yourself royalty. What we don't do however, is understand the steps we need to take to get there. Many teenagers have a clear idea of the job roles they would like when they have finished education, however the focus on the present or the here and now produced through the increased use of the limbic system impacts on their ability to identify the steps required to achieve this ideal. This inability to plan for the future results in adolescents believing they will achieve their goal at some point regardless of the effort they put into education. This lack of focus has a significant impact on motivation and focus in the classroom.

The part of the brain that sparks learning and provides motivation and drive in the adolescent brain is engaged through socialisation and peer approval. If motivation for learning is dependent upon peer approval and socialisation, how are we supposed to motivate our adolescent learners? The answer is actually quite simple. We need to create a learning environment that provides the opportunity for socialisation and positive recognition and approval from their peers.

It is easy to allow ourselves to believe that if we as adults provide high levels of approval and praise, we will be able to meet the neurological needs of our adolescent learners. The focus the limbic system places on relationships and approval is somewhat one sided. The teenage brain does not seek approval from adults but from their peers. Hormones can be held responsible in part for this lack of interest in the opinions of the adults in their lives. During adolescence the hormones in the brain are working in overdrive, heightening emotions while at the same time the brain is strengthening important neurons and synapses, providing the blueprint for deeper thinking and learning. It is through the critical brain development period of adolescence that the brain increases in maturity, develops deeper levels of abstract thinking and makes greater sense of the world. It is during this period the brain begins to develop the thinking mechanisms of an adult brain. While this is happening, hormones are also raging. These two simultaneous events result in both the erratic behaviour often displayed by teenagers and also the lack of respect or interest in the opinions of adults.

Teenagers often appear desperate to grow up and be adults. Many of the behaviours they engage in can be classed as adult behaviours, starting serious relationships, sexual relationships and drinking and partying. The two events taking place in the adolescent brain can be blamed for this. While the deeper levels of thinking and understanding, associated with the adult brain, are developing making the teenagers strive for independence, the overuse of the limbic system results in emotions ruling decision making, resulting in teenagers developing an understanding of adult behaviours yet failing to consider the implications of these. Going out and getting drunk is something adults do so I will do that, no consideration is given to how much alcohol should be consumed or how an individual is going to get home at the end of the night. It is the control these emotions have on decision-making that results to adolescents engaging in risky behaviours (Pickering and Howard-Jones 2007)

5: Teenage behaviour

During the period of adolescence, teenagers often engage in risky behaviours. Drinking, taking drugs, being promiscuous, and engaging in unprotected sex. The easy access teenagers now have to technology has created a whole new range of risky behaviours they now frequently engage in, including sexting, exchanging pornographic images and materials, and developing relationships with strangers.

As discussed in the previous chapter there are various reasons behind the risky behaviours teenagers engage in, including peer pressure and immature emotions. Peer-pressure is without doubt one of the driving influences behind risky behaviour and inappropriate choices made by teenagers. You only have to observe a group of teenagers for a short period of time to witness peer-pressure taking place. If one member of the group starts smoking and then passes the cigarette around the others in the group are likely to follow suit. The more members of the group there are, the more peer-pressure increases often resulting in the most reluctant members of the group to engage in smoking. Sometimes this type of peer-pressure is escalated through the use of verbal abuse or taunting. Name calling often occurs when someone is not willing to participate in the behaviour. Words such as baby, wimp, and chicken and other more demeaning words are often thrown around when trying to convince others to participate in risky behaviours (Pickering and Howard-Jones 2007)

This behaviour is not exclusive to outside the classroom. In the classroom peer-pressure often takes a different appearance. A common problem in the classroom is a disinterested attitude to learning that seems to sweep through the classroom. This is often started by one class member who is regarded highly by other pupils. We often refer to these individuals as popular students. These are the individuals' other students look up to and more often than not want to be like. Once this individual decides the lesson is boring, puts their head on the desk and disengages, others in the classroom will follow this behaviour in the hope of being viewed in the same light as those popular, influential students. Those that do not give in to this peer-pressure are often subjected to name calling and ridicule. Even those students who on the surface appear to have their head in the game and seem focused on learning are going through an internal battle.

As tutors it is often frustrating when we look around our classroom and see disengaged, disinterested learners with their heads on the desk and their thoughts back in the social situation they found themselves in before class. It is particularly disheartening when we feel we have planned a great, fun, engaging lesson and yet find ourselves having to prise answers to questions out of the learners. In these moments it is easy to forget that adolescents are not yet in full control of their emotions, behaviours or reactions to situations that overwhelm them (Adriani and Laviola 2004) It is in these moments when misconceptions that these learners are simply not interested in learning begin to surface and the risk of failing our adolescent learners increases.

There are of course other factors which can heighten and sometimes escalate the risky behaviours, such as having previously been abused, living in an unsafe environment or being in care or "looked after". Evidence suggests young people that fall into these categories are more likely to partake in risky behaviour and are more likely to be exploited in some way. When the adolescent brain stops teenagers from seeing the possible consequences of their actions, be it risky behaviours or simply a lack of interest in education or work, teenagers become resentful of the adults in their lives that try to educate them on the consequences. Teenagers often feel challenged by adults, like they are not being respected or taken seriously but instead are being treated like children. Teenage attitude is viewed as being an expression of feelings and emotions adolescents can control and therefore choose to display. This is far from true. Teenage attitude is a physiological, neurological change taking place within the brain which teenagers have no control over (Crone and Dahl 2012) This fact is one of the most important facts educators of adolescent learners need to truly understand. Without an understanding of this concept, we will never be able to fully support adolescent learners.

There is however, a difference between understanding the

neurological challenges creating this risky behaviour in teenagers and simply allowing it to happen. Understanding the neurological reasoning behind risky and challenging behaviour does not equate to allowing it to happen. Instead, we need to support teenagers in developing those critical thinking skills which will allow them to consider consequences more deeply. This is where the real difficulty in educating teenagers lies. We have just said that teenagers feel challenged when adults attempt to support them in seeing the consequences of certain behaviours so how do we help them develop those critical thinking skills? The answer is simple. Through the way we teach them.

6: Can adolescents learn?

The increased use of the limbic system and the way the different systems do not work together fully in the adolescent brain disrupts the delicate balance between all areas of cognitive importance, with the scales tipping drastically towards the importance of relationships and love (Kozumi 2004) While the adult brain is not all-consumed by the limbic system and the deep range of emotions, it is still influenced by the limbic system. The limbic system is responsible for motivation. Indeed, motivation is emotionally stimulated and regulated. It is our desires for reward that provides motivation.

This is the same in adult and adolescent brains. To complete any task, we need to have some reason for doing it.

It would be ridiculous to suggest that all adults are motivated by the same factor or that all teenagers are motivated by the same reward. While our brains work in a similar pattern, we are still individuals. An Olympic swimmer is motivated by achieving a gold medal at the end of a fantastic swim, this provides the stimulation they need to get into the water every day and train for hours. If you told me I could have a gold medal if I got in the water, I would likely decline. I don't like water and a gold medal does not interest me in the slightest. If you told me I could have a pet Llama if I got in the water, I would probably be straight in there. A Llama is more of a reward to me than a gold medal.

While different factors ignite the limbic system in different individuals, the factors can be categorised. Studies involving MRI's have shown the adult limbic system is engaged by the prospect of future success, including academic success, employment, and life goals. In comparison, the adolescent limbic system is engaged by social factors, including peer approval and romantic relationships (Darmani, Shaddy and Gerdes 1996) The adolescent brain's need for social motivation is focused on the praise, recognition and approval of their peers as opposed to the approval or praise of adults. Teenagers assign value to social acceptance during the period of adolescence, with this overwhelming focus on both peer and romantic relationships resulting in a lack of focus or indeed concern for the future, including academic success or future employment.

Once again, it is easy to view these neurological facts as evidence that teenagers cannot learn effectively. Afterall, you are not going to be focused on mathematic equations when all you can think of is the new relationship you are starting. As adults we have all had moments in our lives where we have found ourselves in meetings or on training courses unable to concentrate due to external factors that we cannot stop thinking about. It is natural to be distracted by our own thoughts, particularly if we have something significant happening in our lives. The difference between adults and adolescents however is that the adult brain has the ability to refocus when needed, the adolescent brain is still developing this essential skill. Surely then, this is further evidence that sometimes teenagers just cannot learn. This is not true. Our adolescent learners just need help directing their focus and staying on task. That is where we, as educators, come in. Our adolescent learners have more than enough ability to learn effectively as long as their learning is guided and supported through effective teaching.

7: The recent history of teaching teenagers

For as long as there has been human life, there has been the teenage years. Indeed, in the early centuries nobody suddenly went from the age of twelve to twenty overnight. Despite this fact, however, the concept of adolescence was not fully recognised until the last two decades of the 19th century. Prior to this, once an individual reached the age of thirteen, they were viewed as an adult. Indeed, in the United Kingdom in early 19th century once individuals reached the period of adolescence, they left education and ventured into the world of work. In 1918 individuals left school at 14, this was increased to 15 in 1957 before reaching the age of 16 in 1972. This age remained the legal age for school leavers until 2013 (DfE 2020).

Today, the thought of thirteen-year-olds being treated the same as adults, provided with the same responsibilities, is enough to send shivers down your spine. This feeling of unease can be attributed to our increased understanding of the development of the adolescent brain. In the same way, we can attribute the lack of care and attention paid to adolescent development and education to the lack of prior knowledge.

Despite the increase in the school leaving age, until the 1980's and beyond, teenagers were still viewed as being young adults, with the main purpose of education being to get the individuals work ready as quickly as possible. Indeed, the concept of further education, while a valid concept, was viewed as an opportunity only available to the elite. Those with money and those with high academic achievements. Secondary schooling was divided, with a small percentage of individuals attending grammar schools. Entry to these more prestigious institutions was based upon an entrance exam. It is important to remember that this exam was not one you could revise for, instead it was similar in fashion to an IQ test. Meaning, regardless of talents, abilities or learning style, if you did not thrive in the prescribed testing environment, you were deemed unlikely to succeed academically and therefore, could not attend grammar school. While this may not seem like a significant fact, individuals attending comprehensive schools left school with lower grades and less achievements than their grammar school counterparts. Indeed, comprehensive schools tended to place an emphasis on vocational subjects to prepare the students for the workforce (Andrews, Hutchinson and Johnes 2016)

Thankfully, the 1980's brought about change within the education sector, with most grammar schools closing by the late 1980's, with the hope of providing all children and teenagers with equal educational opportunities. The reality is, however, that this was not achieved. Indeed, this desire to provide equal opportunities became the very crux of the problem. A blanket approach to education was implemented across all institutions, both primary and secondary, meaning all individuals, regardless of age or stage of neurological development, were taught using the same teaching methods. Copying from textbooks, writing down information passed on by the teachers, were two of the most popular methods for teaching. These methods continued to be popular throughout the 1990's and into the 21st century, with these methods still being used in some educational institutions today. The idea that teenager's brains had neurologically developed to that of an adults influenced the decision to use these somewhat ineffective methods.

Thankfully, a greater understanding of adolescence has been developed throughout the 20th century with hormonal changes and the consequential mood fluctuations now being widely accepted. Despite this, it is only very recently that educators have begun to develop an understanding of the impact these changes can have on an adolescent's ability to effectively learn. The problem with developing your understanding of a topic or concept is that once you have grasped it you need to do something with it. This has proven to not be the case when it comes to teaching the adolescent mind. While we have now accepted the adolescent brain is indeed different to that of an adult, and we are beginning to understand trauma and trauma informed teaching, we still do little to truly engage the adolescent mind and encourage deep learning. We know that adolescent learners like technology so we may throw a bit of technology into our lessons, maybe give them ten minutes to research something online, thus ticking a box on our planning sheets. We might include a class discussion on a topic, but we will make sure we control the narrative, not letting the learners take the discussion in any other way other than what is on our planning! These methods, while seemingly based around the neurological needs of the adolescent learner, are only beneficial to the tutor themselves, allowing them to show variation in their planning and tick those all-important boxes. It does very little for the learners themselves. It will not engage their limbic system and will not result in the deep learning that is so desperately needed. The reality is we, as educators, need to move away from tick box teaching and focus instead on student-led learning.

8: The importance of student led learning

We have discovered that throughout history a top-down, teacher centred approach has always been taken towards teaching and learning. Fortunately, recent advancements in research placed an emphasis on student-led learning, with many researchers stating students should have a choice in their learning, that their opinions and perceptions are relevant Harden and Crosby 2000)

Student led learning is based upon the concept of active learning rather than passive learning. Student led learning provides students with the opportunity to take control of their own learning and development, allowing students to develop a deeper interest in topics, encouraging not only deep learning but also a desire to continue learning outside of the classroom. In an educational world where homework has become a priority with students of all ages being given homework assignments frequently, how wonderful would it be if the students were excited to complete this work? Instead of educators having to ask for homework constantly while listening to a wide variety of excuses as to why it has not yet been completed. Student-led learning requires teachers to alter their perception of their role as an educator, viewing themselves as facilitators of learning rather than a source of knowledge (Kember 1997)

While student led learning is beneficial to students of all ages, it is particularly beneficial in teaching adolescent learners. We have already established during adolescence the brain undergoes a significant pruning process, with the focus on psychological and emotional development and abstract thinking. For abstract thinking to occur, adolescents require opportunities to think deeply, to explore abstract concepts and develop their own opinions and understanding. If teaching is focused on a simple information transaction, with the tutor presenting information without opportunity for exploration or discussion, no abstract thinking can occur. The brain sees no need to do this as all the information required has been provided. How often do we hear phrases such as, "you will need to know this for the exam" or "this needs to be included in your assignment" in the classroom? While we think we are helping our students we are stopping deep learning from taking place. The brain, as we have previously discussed, is an efficient organ, making constant, quick decisions as to what information is important and what is not. Phrases such as these result in the brain deciding the information needs to be stored in the short term for a specific purpose, such as an exam, pruning this information away once the event or purpose has passed. When we change our teaching strategies and engage in student led learning, we provide adolescent learners with the opportunity to engage in deep learning. Asking students challenging and thought-provoking questions without providing answers, allowing discussions to be directed by the students themselves, moving away from the question asked if needed, provides the perfect platform for adolescent learners to explore abstract concepts, and in doing so, engage in deep learning and long-term memory conversion.

There are many challenges within student-led teaching. One of the most significant challenges is allowing students to take the lead while still meeting the requirements of the awarding bodies and the qualifications. Indeed, student-led teaching is more time consuming than traditional teaching methods. Students need to be provided with the time to explore the learning topic, however, as all those working in education are painfully aware of, time is in short supply in most classrooms (Carlson et al 2018) Thankfully, there is a simple solution to this challenge. We need to move away from learning outcome-based lessons. What are learning outcome-based lessons I hear you ask. Learning outcome-based lessons are exactly what they sound like. Lessons focused on a specific learning outcome usually identified in the course handbook. There is a common consensus amongst teachers that if we focus on one of the qualifications learning outcomes each lesson, the students are guaranteed to meet the criteria and achieve their qualification. The rigidity of this approach makes it impossible to provide the students with the time required to truly explore any concepts in depth. Instead, teachers should adopt a more comprehensive approach to learning outcomes and the purpose of each lesson.

Learning outcomes do not need to be taught individually, they also do not need to be the focus of the lesson itself. Learners can easily achieve numerous qualification outcomes in a lesson where the learning outcomes are focused on the learners engaging in research, participating in peer-teaching and exploring a concept in depth (Clapper 2009) Achieving several learning outcomes in each lesson provides the time required for effective student-led teaching to take place.

9: What does teaching teenagers look like?

If we, as educators, have the ability, not to mention responsibility, of getting our adolescent learners to learn, what does our teaching need to look like?

Tutors need to understand the lack of interest or engagement teenagers demonstrate in the classroom is not a true reflection of their desires for the future or their feelings towards education. It is not that teenagers have no aspirations, they do, it is instead a negative result of the over-use of the limbic system.

When we ask teachers and tutors to define teaching, the most common answers are;

1. Giving others information they need
2. Telling students, the information they need to pass a test and gain qualifications

When we ask teachers and tutors to define what their purpose as a teacher or tutor is, the most common answers are;

1. To get students to gain a qualification so they can get a job
2. Help students pass a test

When we ask teachers and tutors what the biggest challenges are when teaching teenagers, the most common answers are;

1. The lack of respect they show
2. The lack of interest they show in class, they don't listen and are too busy talking to each other

Our role as teachers and tutors is not to teach to the test, it is not to impart onto the learners the basic information they need to pass an exam or gain a qualification. The reality is teachers are not really needed for any of that. There is nothing you need to gain a qualification that you cannot access online. It is easy in today's world to search the internet for the information you need to pass an exam or write an essay. This rules out the top two answers teachers provide when asked what teaching is and what the purpose of teachers is. If our role is not to get students to pass tests or achieve qualifications, then what is it? Qualifications and exam results are what students are in education for, isn't it?

The short answer to that question is yes, however it is not so clear cut. Education is without doubt about achievement and progression; however, achievement and progression does not automatically mean pieces of paper stamped by an awarding body. Progression and achievement take many forms including developing self-confidence and self-belief, making friends, time-management skills, improving on and developing academic skills regardless of whether pass marks are met or not, critical and deep thinking and independence. When we support our learners in developing these skills, the qualification becomes somewhat insignificant and learners often achieve this without really realising how hard they have worked because learning has been focused on their own achievements and self-worth and not on a course handbook. Our learners should leave us being better than we are.

Teaching is not about imparting knowledge on learners but rather about supporting them to build those all-important skills they need to find out that knowledge for themselves. Teaching is about igniting that desire to learn in each student in a way that allows them to truly learn information and retain it, allowing it to have an impact on their lives after leaving education. Those of us working in secondary or further education are often the last line of defence for adolescent learners; the last ones to ensure the desire to learn is ignited. It is a huge responsibility and one we must get right. If teaching to you is standing in front of a class of students dictating information to them then I am afraid you are in the wrong job.

You can have amazingly detailed schemes of work and colour-coded lesson plans. You can know the course handbook inside out but none of this will make you a great teacher or inspire the students to learn. The most effective and beneficial lessons are not planned around a course handbook. Learning outcomes are not simply copy and pasted from the course specification. Instead, learning outcomes are planned around the needs of the learners and should be focused on supporting learners to develop those important skills that engage the correct systems within the brain and ignite deep, effective learning.

The next question we need to consider is what does a learning environment look like to you? The most common answers are:

1. Calm and quiet
2. An environment with no distractions such as mobile phones or music

While it is easy to see the benefits of having a calm, quiet and distraction free learning environment there is often a clear difference between what adult's view as being a calm, quiet environment and what adolescent learners view as calm and quiet. We need to remember that adolescents growing up in today's society have never truly experienced a quiet environment. Their world is never silent. In today's society teenagers live with earphones in their ears. You only have to walk down the street and any adolescent walking on their own will have some form of headphones on and will be listening to music. When they are not doing this, they are often in large groups, talking and often shouting. Very often, teenagers have constant noise in the background when they are at home doing homework or doing nothing at all, which seems to be a favourite hobby of many teenagers. Their brains are so used to being in a noisy environment that they very often tune out much of the background noise. When you remove that noise and put teenagers in a silent environment learning, concentration and focus can become more difficult as the brain attempts to adjust to what is essentially a new environment.

We are often under the misconception that the best learning environment is one that is quiet, where the learners have their heads down and are studiously writing and taking notes, so engaged in their work and learning that they are not conversing with their friends or even the teacher. To put it simply, this is wrong and if we are using this misconception as a basis for our teaching practice and the way we manage our classrooms we are once again failing. A truly effective learning environment is one full of conversation and discussion, one where critical thinking skills are extended and ideas explored. Real learning does not take place at a desk, it occurs through discussion and exploration, hands-on learning and real-life experiences (Luna 2004)

The traditional learning environment is one that aims to remove individuality, expecting learners to conform to one specific form of learning, usually sitting in silence and note-taking. Removing individuality is demotivating for anyone, adults and adolescents alike, it is however more detrimental to adolescents. During the period of adolescent development teenagers are trying to figure out who they are and where they fit in in the world. This applies to education. Teenagers are trying to figure out where they sit within the academic world, what their strengths and weaknesses are and most importantly what their likes and passions are. When we remove individuality from the classroom, we stifle the learner's ability to discover their passions and we fail to meet their needs.

The need for individuality also applies to target setting. Once again targets are viewed as being yet another document that needs completing each term to tick a box with very little consideration or thought going into each target. Often targets seem somewhat generic with all learners having a target for attendance or completing the course. The question we need to ask ourselves is are these really targets? Completing the course is surely something we expect all our students to achieve so why are we setting this as a target? Targets are there to inspire and drive learners forward in their learning. Attendance and completion targets do nothing to inspire. Targets should instead be based on the individual goals and needs of the learners. If a learner lacks confidence in public speaking a target should be set around this.

10: Poverty and the adolescent brain

Although studies into the direct link between poverty and brain structure are relatively recent, two significant studies have shown the effects of poverty on brain structure. Children and young people growing up in poverty have reduced grey matter volumes in the frontal and temporal cortex (Blair and Raver 2016) An examination of 283 MRI's found children and adolescents from poor backgrounds, with a low socioeconomic status have a thinner or under-developed prefrontal cortex compared to their more affluent peers. With the prefrontal cortex playing an important part in executive functioning it comes as little surprise that children with low socioeconomic status have lower levels of academic achievement.

Socioeconomic disparities in school readiness and academic performance are well documented, with evidence showing children living in deprived areas have a consistently low level of academic attainment. With this low level of academic attainment continuing through childhood, adolescence, and adulthood (Hair et al 2015)

Poverty is often a cycle running through generations and is difficult to break. There is a prominent link between parental educational attainment and that of their children. Research has shown that children whose parents are educated to degree level, or higher, have greater levels of academic achievement than those children whose parents have not attained this level of education. The common assumption is that highly educated parents develop a greater understanding of the importance of education, influencing the way they interact with their children as well as the educational opportunities they provide their children with. In contrast, parents without this level of education, particularly those with a low socio-economic status, often view themselves as being less academic, often referring to themselves as 'thick.' This belief then becomes a self-fulfilling prophecy in which an individual tells themselves something about their own self enough times that they begin not only to believe it but to also physically demonstrate these beliefs. This self-fulfilling prophecy not only changes an individual's belief's but also the structure of their brain. When individuals believe they cannot do something they stop trying, resulting in neuroplasticity pruning away the required skills.

Parental qualifications also create demographic characteristics. Studies would suggest education determines where individuals live, whom they marry, their income and the number of children an individual is likely to have. These demographic characteristics directly influence the neighbourhoods in which children live (Eccles and Davis-Keen 2005) Residential neighbourhoods categorised as impoverished are more likely to experience violence, crime and police presence, with these factors increasing neural stressors. There is a significant link between poverty and increased stress indicators in the brain. Some of this is often easily explained away in relation to adults, external factors associated with poverty and a low socioeconomic status, including finances, housing issues and the ever-increasing cost of living, increases corticosterone in the brain. While we may be able to provide some explanation for the stress indicators in the adult brain it does not account for the same increased stressors in young children and adolescents. Indeed, increased amounts of corticosterone are found in children and young people living in poverty. Further studies have suggested these increased stressors are a direct result of the environment on the brain, with increased background noise and exposure to family arguments playing a significant role in this. Increased corticosterone alters the neural activity within the brain, indeed, the increased stressors alter neural activity, pathways and connections in such a way that the brain begins to associate anxiety and stress with reactive or defensive behaviours, stopping reflective behaviour from taking place.

Adolescents living in poverty and areas of high deprivation often display disruptive behaviour. This once again can be attributed to the additional stressors and increase in stress hormones. As previously discussed, the developing adolescent brain increases the use of the limbic system, heightening emotions, including feelings of anxiety, fear and frustration. The additional stressors created through poverty further heighten these emotions, particularly the emotion of fear. It is important to remember that not only is the fear emotion intensified during the period of adolescence, it is also associated with experiences, situations and thoughts that we as adults may not view as fearful.

While parental education and neighbourhood demographics play a role in lower-level academic attainment in children living in poverty, there are various other factors which can be identified as attributing factors. As we established earlier the early years are, alongside the period of adolescence, critical in brain development. The effects of poverty on the brain start in early childhood with young children living in poverty making up a significant percentage of children defined as developmentally at risk, thus requiring early intervention. These children are often behind their peers developmentally, specifically in language and emotional development (Kappen 2007)

Studies have shown children living in poverty are exposed to less language than their more affluent peers. There are many theories and arguments as to why this is, one such argument being that parents with low socioeconomic status often work long hours or more than one job, reducing the amount of time spent with their young children. Often young children are left in the care of a relative or friend instead of attending childcare settings due to rising costs, despite the funding now being made available to low-income families.

Another argument is that of limited vocabulary exposure. Indeed, over recent years the concept of 'the word gap' has been explored in greater detail, highlighting clear disparities between children with a low socio-economic status and their more affluent peers. Research has shown young children living in poverty learn four words fewer a day than their peers and have fewer opportunities to speak a day than children of a higher socio-economic status (Kurchirko 2017) There is often a common misconception that a delay in language development will only impact that specific area of development, posing problems in relation to communication. This could not be further from the truth. Language development provides a foundation for all other forms of learning. Indeed, without effective language development effective learning cannot take place. Language allows children to develop an understanding of verbal content and to absorb written information prevalent to learning. How can we expect children to sit in a classroom and learn historical facts when they do not have an understanding of the basic vocabulary. Language development also plays a significant role in behaviour. To understand our emotions, we need to first be able to express them. This requires a certain level of language maturity. When language maturity is lacking, emotions are often displayed negatively.

The neurological changes poverty and a low socio-economic status creates an attitude amongst educators that adolescents that have experienced these neurological changes are somewhat uneducable, are not worth the effort provided to those learners, many of whom are more affluent, that display a better attitude towards learning and education. This has resulted in years of poor education for those teenagers living in poverty, increasing the low attainment rates, and perpetuating the cycle of low attainment through generations. There are significant failings in further education in relation to supporting those living in poverty. Instead of taking the time to truly develop an understanding of this demographic and develop strategies that will best support these students, we continue to label them as disruptive students, viewing them as being poor in academia resulting in no stretch and challenge. Instead, we enrol students on courses we feel they are most suited to, often low-level courses, providing them with no aspirations for success, often expecting them to fail. Unfortunately, many do fail and do not complete these courses. There are two identified reasons for this, the first one being we enrol these students on courses we feel are suitable for them, not on courses they have a true interest in. Secondly, we fail to address the basic needs of the students, failing to accept that some students come to further education colleges without the basic skills required for effective learning.

We, as educators and learning establishments, need to move away from this stereotypical behaviour and instead address the different neurological needs of this specific demographic of learner. Meeting these differing neurological needs, alongside meeting the equally challenging neurological changes of the adolescent brain, can seem daunting and even impossible, but I can assure you it is not. It simply requires a longer process. This specific demographic of learner first needs to develop the skills needed to learn effectively, not just those basic academic skills, such as Maths and English, but the skills required to better manage their fight or flight emotions, lowering the stress factors within their brains, better preparing them for effective learning in the future. The reality is, until the impact of poverty and low socioeconomic status on neuroplasticity within the adolescent brain, this demographic of learner cannot engage in deep learning, and we, as educators, will continue to fail them.

11: Socialisation

The concept of socialisation in the classroom can be one that strikes fear into a teacher's heart. Socialisation in the classroom brings about images of a loud classroom with students sitting on desks, chatting with their peers about their plans for the weekend, celebrities or where they are going for lunch. Teenagers are naturally rather chatty with each other. Remember this is all to do with that pesky limbic system and the need for peer approval and relationships. An interesting observation can often be made in a classroom full of adolescent learners, conversations flow and the noise levels increase when learners have the freedom to discuss whatever it is they are finding interesting in their lives at the moment with their peers, in fact it is difficult to get them to stop talking, yet as soon as the teacher asks a question relating to the lesson everyone has lost the ability to speak. You can almost see the tumbleweed blowing by as the teacher waits for a reply while the learners avoid making eye contact. Part of this sudden inability to speak that engulfs all adolescent learners as soon as a question is posed can be blamed on the need for peer-approval and the overthinking nature of the adolescent brain. When the teacher asks a question panic sets in in the adolescent brain. Not because they don't know the answer, they very well may do, but because they have a fear of giving the wrong answer. This fear is not based on what the teacher might say if they give an incorrect answer but rather the reactions they may receive from their peers. We all fear being laughed at or ridiculed but during those teenage years this fear is heightened to a point where teenagers would rather appear less academic, even accepting poor report cards or parents' evenings, to ensure they are not ridiculed by their peers and that they fit in. If our adolescent students do not want to engage in discussions relating to the lesson topic instead to keep their socialisation planted firmly in the realm of reality TV, celebrities and social media, how can we possibly make socialisation a part of our teaching and learning?

Socialisation and learning are viewed as two polar opposites. Socialisation conjures up images of fun and excitement. Spending time with friends and family, laughing and engaging in activities we find fun. Learning on the other hand conjures up images of classrooms and desks, of notetaking and silence and of boredom. For teaching and learning to be effective we need to blend these two seemingly opposite concepts together. Socialisation, by definition, means mixing socially with others. What socialisation should entail is very much open to interpretation.

The concept of using socialisation as a teaching and learning method is a simple one; let them talk to each other. Obviously, conversations about social media or the latest gossip do not hold any value in relation to learning, the challenge is to get our adolescent learners talking about the lesson content. The first thing we need to do is remove the constant barrage of questions, both open and directed. Questioning is an important technique in teaching, but it is only effective when it is used in the right place and in the right context. Having direct questioning on your lesson plan might tick boxes for observations and audits but that is the only benefit if questions are not used effectively. We need to replace teacher questioning with peer questioning. We need the learners to be asking questions to each other, opening the pathway for deep discussion and sustained shared thinking. If learners are truly engaged in the topic and in their learning, they will hold discussions with each other relating to their learning. That pressure to simply answer a question and get it correct in front of a large classroom of peers is removed and if the learners are comfortable with each other and have worked with each other previously they are more likely to share ideas regardless of their confidence levels in their ideas or answers being correct Remember to learn, the brain needs to be motivated and the limbic system needs to be ignited, socialisation with each other is igniting this process.

As tutors there is a fear of losing control of our classrooms. There is a worry that if we give our adolescent learners freedom to work with each other, to communicate and talk to each other the learners will allow both their minds and their conversations to wander. This will make it difficult for us as tutors to bring the learners back to the lesson, to regain focus and produce any real, effective learning. The reality is, while there will always be an element of risk that the learners will stray from the task set and discuss other things there is also a strong possibility the learners will stay engaged when they are provided with the trust and opportunity to lead their own learning. The truth is we will never stop learners from straying from learning topics. It is almost impossible for a learner to give one hundred percent engagement in a lesson that lasts for three hours. Teenagers are not alone in this; I can think of many occasions when I have been on training courses and my mind has wandered off to Asda to think about my shopping list for the week. I am sure I am not alone in this. Our brains are complex organisms at whatever age.

The key here is getting the balance between independent learning and adult intervention. The concept of allowing adolescent learners to work with each other, to socialise and discuss the learning topic is not an invitation for the tutor to grab a brew and put their feet up for thirty minutes. Tutors need to remain constantly engaged in the lesson, regardless of whether they are stood at the front of the class presenting or providing learners with opportunities to work independently or in groups. Walking around the room and checking in with the different groups is important, but don't be surprised if the conversation and discussion dries up while you are there. If a group is struggling, help give them some points to consider to get the conversation going. It is important once you have done this that you move away. The learners need time to digest the points and begin a conversation with each other. If you are hovering over them like an army chopper, they are going to be far too concerned with wanting to provide you with the correct answers than to engage in an in-depth discussion. One of the key elements and something which I think many tutors struggle with at times is making sure we do not take over or lead the discussion. When you are helping a group get their ideas off the ground or you have been graciously allowed to participate in the discussions of a more confident group the temptation is always there to lead the discussions. As tutors we always have the learning outcomes at the forefront of our minds, we know where we need the learners to be knowledge wise by the end of the session. At times it can seem like the learners are digressing from where we want them to be and are taking the conversations in a different direction. Our natural reaction to this is to interrupt and dive on in with various lines of questioning in an attempt to bring the conversations and discussions back to where we think they should be. Far from being helpful this approach can actually be detrimental to learning in a few different ways. Firstly, there will always be a reason why the learners have seemingly digressed from the original question, moving beyond the original question and exploring further concepts is a sign that discussions are happening, and a deeper level of learning is taking place. Far from being disengaged in the original question the learners are actually so engaged in it they are wanting to look at it from a different angle or they have stumbled upon something relating to the topic which has interested and intrigued them. If we wade in and stop this discussion, we are stopping further deep learning from taking place. Adolescent learners will also see this as a sign that they should not be thinking for themselves in the classroom.

Assignments. The word all students, and let's be honest many teachers, hate. For decades the word assignment has been associated with long, written essays, deadlines, and often copious amounts of stress. As teachers and tutors we spend our summers producing our assessment timetables, deciding which criteria will fit into which essay and by the end of the summer we have planned for our learners to complete a written assignment each week. Once term starts, we complain each week about the amount of marking we have to do. The question we all need to ask ourselves are who are all these written assignments benefitting? They are not benefitting the learners. They are not benefitting us as teachers and tutors. So why are we doing them? I think the answer is because it is safe. Written assessments are proven in the sense that awarding bodies have always accepted written assessments as proof of understanding and written assignments are viewed as being easy to mark and provide written feedback. Written assignments are a way of saying, "look I taught them this topic and they understood it." On the surface this may appear to be true but if we look a little deeper it becomes apparent that learning is not really taking place. Students may be producing work that demonstrates an understanding but if you ask them a week or two later what they wrote in their assignment they will struggle to tell you. This is because deep learning rarely takes place when teenagers are simply writing down the information the tutor has told them they need to include, usually using notes and PowerPoints provided by the tutor. It almost becomes rote learning, just like teaching to the test. Let's not forget, adolescent learners need socialisation to learn. Written assignments and assessments do not provide opportunities for this.

There are many different assessment methods that can be used which provide teenage learners with the opportunity to socialise and work in groups while still meeting the qualification requirements. Project assignments are a great way to not only allow adolescent learners to interact and work with their peers but also allow deeper learning to take place. Project learning also removes the conveyor belt culture of written assignments that is constantly running in educational settings. Setting projects allow tutors to pull together all the criteria required to develop an understanding of a particular topic, providing more of an opportunity for adolescent learners to delve into a topic more deeply, discuss all aspects of the topic with their peers, sharing ideas and opening new lines of enquiry and investigation for the learners to navigate. Project work also requires learners to continuously re-visit and review previous work supporting the process of synapses strengthening, helping information be converted to long-term memory, resulting in deep and effective learning taking place.

With relationships playing such an essential role in the adolescent brain, and in the adolescent brain ability to learn, we need to consider the relationship between tutor and students. While the teenage brain places more importance on peer relationships than relationships with adults, it is still important that we as tutors get the relationship correct. For decades the relationship between tutors / teachers and their students has been one of imbalance, taking a hierarchical approach with teachers / tutors being both viewed as and viewing themselves as superior to the students. While the concept of the teacher dictating and the students listening and note-taking seems somewhat archaic it is still prominent in teaching today, particularly in secondary and further education institutions. While we are not taught in teacher training that we as teachers or tutors are superior in some way to our students, we are told to almost demand respect. During teacher training we are told we need to command the classroom, develop some sort of authoritative presence. We learn behaviour management strategies and are often told to 'set out our stall' at the beginning of the year, enforce the rules and make those learners respect you. I suppose the question we need to ask ourselves here is why? Why do we feel we have a right to do that? What gives us the right to demand respect? How often have you heard teachers tell teenage students respect is earned not given? I don't think I can count the times. Yet we expect to just be given respect without giving any back.

This hierarchical approach to teaching has a detrimental impact on the type and strength of relationship built between teacher / tutor and the adolescent learners. An effective relationship requires perfect balance. How do we create this level of perfect balance? The answer is pretty simple. Talk to them. The key word here is 'to' and not 'at'. Talking to them means listening to what they have to say and respecting their opinions regardless of whether you agree with them or not. Get to know your students. Knowing your students involves more than just knowing their name and any additional learning needs they may have. Truly knowing your learners means getting to know them at a personal level, learning what inspires your learners, what their difficulties are, not just inside the classroom but also in their lives outside of those four walls. It doesn't take a great deal of time to ask your students what they did at the weekend, to remember that they have siblings or that they are in a romantic relationship with someone. Knowing these details allows you to engage in conversations with your learners that relate to topics other than learning. Remember the adolescent brain, just like the adult brain, creates a need for validation. As humans we want to feel that we are important, valued and that our voices are listened to. As an adult, I often feel frustrated when I don't feel like my voice is being listened to. Adolescents are not exempt from this; in fact, their emotions are heightened so they actually feel that frustration on a much higher scale. This equal balance also requires us as teachers to give something back. For any relationship to be truly effective both parties need to be involved equally. We need to share parts of our lives with the learners too, to help them see that actually we are human and we have lives outside of the classroom.

Obviously, the information we share needs to be appropriate and the relationships we build with our students need to stay professional and within those important professional boundaries. Sharing information about yourself and your life does not mean you have to give out your address, phone number and invite your students round to meet your family. It means letting them know you have a family; you can tell your students you have children without sharing names or even ages if you don't want to. I have often found sharing stories from my younger days is a great way to get the learners to view me as something more than just a tutor, although I do think that sometimes they begin to view me as less of a teacher and more of a fossil, particularly when I tell them I didn't have a mobile phone when I was growing up. I have before heard a student ask a teacher if they had had their hair done because it looked lighter to which the teacher replied, "my hair is nothing to do with you, or this lesson." It was obvious she had been to the hair salon so why not just say so? The learner was taking an interest and opening up a dialogue that could strengthen that all important student / tutor relationship but instead the tutor closed it down, making themselves once again appear like some strange enigma that is a world apart from the learners themselves and not someone with whom they could ever relate to. In recent years I have had conversations ranging from relationships to fake tan and everything in between. I know my learners and they know me, and I have always found I get far more out of them when I have a positive relationship with them than if I don't. Positive relationships with students do not only support effective learning but also play an important role in safeguarding. Teenagers are more likely to share information relating to safeguarding if they feel that they can relate to you.

12: Technology

While the desire for social and peer approval is a direct result of neurological changes within the brain due to hormones and brain development, it is also greatly influenced by technology. Technology, particularly the easy, frequent access adolescents have to smart phones and the access this provides for access to social media platforms, provides greater opportunities for teenagers to be social and engage with their peers. This further engages the limbic system. If you ask any teacher or tutor what they feel is one of the biggest factors in disengaged students they will most likely say mobile phones. They have quickly become a pain in the posterior for those working in education. This is not a new phenomenon, it started well before the introduction of smart phones.

I can clearly remember attending school in the nineties and noughties when mobile phones became a thing. I remember getting my Nokia 3310 and feeling like a superstar at school. Not entirely sure why I felt like that as most people had one. The Nokia 3310 was far from a smart phone. There was no touch screen, no access to social media (it didn't even exist at this point), you only had so many characters per text message which brought about text language, and cameras on phones were still a distant dream. Despite what now seems rather archaic technology, I do believe there is actually a Nokia 3310 in a technology museum, it still changed the way adolescents thought and behaved and it was still an issue in classroom engagement. Everyone was trying to text their friends under the table, with these friends often being sat a few seats away. Mobile phones and texting replaced throwing notes to each other. Rules for mobile phones came out, including not having them out in the classroom and a whole school ban on bringing mobile phones to school was enforced.

The introduction and development of social media has

increased the dependency on mobile phones tenfold. Mobile phones and social media platforms are now the main source of communication between adolescents, they form and maintain friendships using these platforms. There are arguments amongst both theorists and teachers that the use of mobile phones and technology has created disengaged, distracted learners, with low levels of concentration. (Blakemore and Mills 2014) This argument has resulted in teachers and tutors attempting to remove mobile phones from the classroom. Over recent years I have seen, and tried, various methods to remove this technology from the classroom. I have seen various classrooms with a mobile phone box at the front of the class, with each student having to deposit their mobile device upon arrival. This is usually closely monitored by the teacher, with their hawk eyes checking every student makes a phone deposit. You can hear the cries of "I haven't got my phone," and "this is stupid," echoing through the corridors. Then there is the strategy of peer pressure. "If one person gets their phone out you all have to put them on the desk at the front." Inevitably a student forgets the no phone rule and is instead overcome with the need to check their phone, resulting in arguments, complaints and insults as the other students reluctantly make their way to the front of the classroom to be relieved of their mobile devices. This usually takes a good ten to fifteen minutes. All of which is time taken out of the lesson, reducing learning time and counteracting the very purpose of the mobile phone ban, making it a pointless, time-consuming exercise.

It is important to remember that technology and a technological world is the domain in which our adolescents are being brought up in. For many they have never experienced a world without smart phones, social media or Netflix. Google has always been available at the click of a button and taking selfies is simply a way of life. Using technology is not something our teenagers consciously think about, it is simply a habit. The pruning process that takes place through neuroplasticity, with repeated experiences strengthening neurons supports the benefits of implementing technology in teaching, the constant use of technology, mobile phones and social media has resulted in stronger neurological pathways which when used correctly can increase deeper learning. Technology in the classroom is not a new concept, it is actually one that has been around for many, many years and has continued to evolve over the decades. If I close my eyes now, I can still see the words *to All Things Bright And Beautiful,* being projected onto the wall in the school assembly hall, usually somewhat lopsided but I can still remember the excitement of being the one chosen to move the acetate up the projector during the hymn. In primary school nothing said "I've made it," more than being responsible for the over-head projector. We have been using technology as a teaching tool for decades, we are just more aware of it now because our students no longer have to wait their turn to be projector king or queen, instead they have technology in the palm of their hand all day, every day.

The value of technology as a tool for learning has been recognised over recent years, with many efforts being made to incorporate technology into the learning environment. It is almost impossible now to find a classroom that does not have an interactive smartboard. We have ICT suites, iPad and laptops. Some educational institutions have virtual reality software. Technology is in every classroom. The problem with technology isn't a lack of access, but rather how or why it is used. In many classrooms interactive boards are used in one of two ways, as a posher version of a chalkboard which tutors just write information on for the students to copy down or as a device on which they can show their PowerPoint. The interactive part is all but forgotten in most classrooms. We give the learners iPad or tablets in the lesson and set a research task, believing we are using ICT resources in a way that benefits the learners and supports the lesson. In reality, the learners quickly google the research question, pull up the first website that comes up before starting a conversation with their peers about a topic not related to the lesson. The students may be using technology, but they are not really engaging with it.

On the flip side we have classrooms that rely completely on technology as a teaching tool. As tutors we all find new platforms for teaching and learning we like and feel our students really engage well with. Exploration of technology as a teaching tool increased dramatically throughout the Covid 19 pandemic when teaching moved online and many, if not most, tutor and teachers have found online teaching platforms and tools they like. Surely this is a good thing, is it not? If adolescents learn better when using technology, we are on to a winner. Wrong. Teenagers do engage in learning when using technology but only when it is used correctly. We now face a problem of over reliance on technology. It's a bit like when you hear a song you really like, you play it constantly and even find yourself singing it randomly throughout the day until eventually you become so used to hearing it that it just becomes background noise. The same thing happens when we rely on one piece of technology or one learning platform week in week out in every lesson because we know the learners enjoyed it the first few times we used it. Using the platform becomes routine for the learners and they start to just go through the motions of using the platform without any real conscious effort.

It is important that we do not become reliant on one resource, platform, or way of teaching. While the use of technology in teaching is important when teaching adolescent learners in this modern, technology driven world, it must be varied, exciting and engaging. If we are relying on one platform in the same way we once relied on a PowerPoint, we are still not fully engaging the learners and we are continuing to do them a disservice. If learners are using technology in the same way they used to use note taking, they are not learning effectively. As tutors and teachers, we need to be using technology and devices that the learners are familiar with, which ignite their limbic system and kick start the learning process in their brains. Love them or hate them we need to be willing to allow mobile phones to be used in the classroom. Using mobile phones in the classroom does not mean giving the learners free reign to snapchat, Instagram and text away till their hearts are content, it means engaging learners in activities that use their phones in such a way that the learners have neither time nor inclination to use social media.

13: Fast-paced environment

My own research study identified increased engagement during the lesson as well as greater overall achievements and outcomes when lessons were varied and quick-paced.

Quick-paced does not mean skipping lesson content or only exploring information at a surface level, the quality and content of your lesson should not be diminished by a faster paced lesson.

Increasing the pace of your lesson and including a variety of activities and resources allows you to explore content in greater detail and from different angles.

A quick-paced environment is one that contains various teaching methods and activities, including group work, discussions, technology, photography and creative tasks. Lessons should not be based around only one activity but should contain a variety of activities that continuously challenge the learners cognitive thinking and re-engage the limbic system in the adolescent brain. The more times we can ignite a strong reaction within the limbic system the more likely it is that deeper learning will take place.

The adolescent brain requires a learning environment that is engaging and quick-paced and should provide adolescent learners with the freedom to not only cognitively explore their learning but to do so within a social interaction required for the overactive limbic system to be stimulated and for the adolescent brain to engage in deep, effective learning.

It is important to remember the hormonal and chemical changes taking place in the adolescent brain reduce the level of focus taking place. The limbic system is constantly pulling the teenage brain's focus back to emotions and relationships, both romantic relationships and social relationships with their peers, making long periods of concentration difficult to achieve. We have all sat through seminars or training courses and had our minds wander.

Not only do our adolescent learners require a fast-paced environment, they also require fast-paced feedback. We have already established teenagers need instant gratification and reward due to their inability to truly think beyond the here and now. Pages and pages of written feedback given to the learners two weeks after they handed in an assignment is ineffective. Most learners have a quick skim over the sheet to see if they have met the desired criteria and passed the assignment, once they see that they have they shove the assignment and feedback into a folder and forget all about it, with both the assignment and the feedback never seeing the light of day again. While we as adults find receiving written feedback rewarding teenagers do not. It is unlikely they will remember the full content of the assignment that has been graded and will therefore pay little attention to the feedback provided. The very purpose of feedback is to provide learners with guidance and goals for future work and personal development, for it to be truly effective we must provide it in a way that engages the adolescent brain, in a quick, fast-paced method.

Verbal feedback during activities serves two purposes. Firstly, it provides learners with the knowledge that they are working well whilst also providing learners with a sense of acknowledgment and confidence in their own abilities. We all like to be told we have done something well. Positive praise stimulates the same area of our brain that is stimulated by receiving money or romantic relationships. As we have already established relationships and the desire for these takes up a significant portion of adolescent thinking, stimulating this area re-engages and re-focuses the adolescent brain on the task they are completing. When we continuously stimulate this area of the brain, we allow neuroplasticity to take place, resulting in the adolescent brain associating completed work with positive feelings, increasing the likelihood of work being completed and submitted.

Verbal feedback does not only include formative feedback but also summative. Have you ever noticed how adolescents always seem to have earphones in? Listening to music, talking on the phone to their friends, watching videos, all carried out while using earphones. Not only are adolescent learners more likely to engage in verbal feedback in the classroom but they are also more likely to engage in summative feedback if they have the option to listen to it rather than read it. There are various methods that can be used to provide verbal feedback including phone and computer Apps or just simple voice recorders. Verbal feedback can then be uploaded to whichever online platform is used for work submission.

14: Real-life experiences

Various studies and pieces of research have made connections between adolescent engagement and real-life experiences (Koepp et al 1998) As teachers and tutors we sometimes forget that the adolescents we are teaching are becoming young adults and as such have their own thoughts, feelings and opinions as well as a desire to have these validated. Capturing the adolescent brain's attention and maintaining it long enough for deep, successful learning to take place creativity, novelty and ever-changing teaching methods are required.

Findlay (2014) stated the very nature of the adolescent brain, particularly the adolescent brain that is surrounded by and constantly engaged with technology, has a 'popcorn brain' construction, with this neurological phenomenon being a direct result of the ability adolescents now have to switch between devices, platforms and conversations quickly. Providing real experiences not only allows the learners to understand abstract concepts, it also allows the learners to link the concept they are trying to understand to an actual experience, linking memories of physical movement and a written or verbal concept. The more experiences the brain has of a specific topic, activity or situation the stronger the neural pathways become, strengthening memory and information retention. The more the brain experiences something the more the brain realises the importance of the information.

The increased use in the limbic system and the focus this places on emotions, relationships and the opinions of their peers has a direct impact on their ability to learn. How many times have we heard parents, teachers or just adults in general say that teenagers are selfish, self-absorbed and think of no one but themselves? I can almost hear the collective moan of parents across the country as the teenager leaves their cereal bowl on the side instead of putting it in the dishwasher or steps over items left on the stairs to be taken up too engrossed in their mobile devices or in their own minds to even consider helping out and taking the items upstairs. It is a common occurrence and has been for generations. It is true that during the period of adolescence teenagers are self-absorbed and self-focused. The thing we fail to consider when we are calling teenagers selfish is the lack of control they have over this behaviour. The self-focus teenagers experience is not a conscious effort. They do not make a conscious decision to ignore the dishes that need washing or to forget to put their laundry in the basket despite being asked five times, they just struggle to process the information which results in them forgetting. The things that are going on in their lives take precedent over their thoughts, feelings and actions. The adolescent brain is trying to make sense of the world around them, develop the concept of abstract thinking and develop a sense of independence all while trying to learn, develop and demonstrate some level of maturity. If a subject, concept or idea does not relate to their here and now, they struggle to focus on it. Concepts they have no experience in or ideas that seem historic fail to engage the limbic system, resulting in missed opportunities to learn. Learning material needs to be made relevant and relatable to the learners. They need to be able to make connections between their own lives, experiences, and the content of the learning material. This may seem like an impossible task, especially if the learning content is not something that appears to relate to the life of a teenager however anything can be made relevant. If the subject is history and you are exploring World War Two, ask the learners to imagine what it would be like if World War Two had happened in today's world or consider how their lives would have been different if the outcome of the war had been different. Make it relatable to them.

15: Think Four Approach

Now we have developed a basic understanding of the adolescent brain and have explored some of the key strategies that can be used to engage the adolescent brain in learning, we need to figure out how often we should use these strategies and how many we should use in each lesson. The answer is simple. All of them. Every lesson. When planning lessons, 'Think Four'. Think Four is the process of including all four strategies in each lesson. Incorporating technology, socialisation, real-life experiences into a fast-paced learning environment provides the best environment for adolescent learners to effectively learn in.

The Think Four approach is not a one-off lesson approach to be tried once and then cast aside, or to only be included in lessons where observations are being held. Instead, it needs to be an approach which is consistently embedded in all teaching and learning. It is important to remember, as with all changes, new strategies can take time to be fully embedded and it will invariably take more than one session for the learners to adapt to the new ways of learning, to develop an understanding of the new freedoms the Think Four approach provides, and to learn how to manage this new freedom in a way which supports their learning. Learners will, without doubt, push the boundaries of this new approach to start with. They may discuss topics during discussions which are not relevant, they may access Apps on their phones that are not supportive of the lesson. In fact, they most likely will. In these situations, you simply need to get them back on track, bring the discussion back to the topic and keep working hard to engage them. Neuroplasticity is an amazing thing but it is not an instant process. It takes time and we have to be willing as tutors to invest in that time. Throwing in the towel when you hit the first hurdle will neither benefit you nor the learners. We attempt to instil in our learner's resilience and perseverance, yet we often lack these traits ourselves within our teaching. It is human nature to fear change. We are naturally creatures of habit and comfort, change, just like learning, stimulates neuroplasticity and changes in the brain. These changes result in increased hormones and noradrenaline. We all fear failure. This fear can often result in a failure to take a risk or make a change. While this may make us, as educators, feel secure, it has a significant adverse effect on our learners, the very people we are there to support, the very purpose of our careers. If we are so willing to let our learners down rather than place ourselves in a situation that may make us feel uncomfortable it may be time to ask ourselves if teaching is the right job for us.

So now we have decided to overcome our fears and do what is best for our learners, it's time to consider the best ways to truly implement the Think Four approach. Let's start with that initial engagement. When learners walk into the classroom, they are more often than not either talking, using their mobile phones or a combination of both. To engage learners from the very start we need to harness their current actions, making learning a simple continuation of their previous activity. An effective way to do this is to have a task or activity involving technology and their mobile phones as a starter activity, allowing learners to move seamlessly from social media to a learning platform.

This also provides the perfect opportunity for socialisation, learners can discuss the task with their peers, either verbally or using the technology. This type of starter activity also allows for the class stragglers to arrive. If we are all honest, while we expect and often demand our learners be in class on time, there are very few occasions when this happens. Having a starter activity set up, that is self-explanatory ensures engagement of all learners, including those that have arrived late. Five minutes into the lesson and we have already hit two of the four requirements.

16: Best outcomes for the learners

Before we dive into this final chapter, I would ask you to keep one question in your mind as you read. "Why do I teach?" What makes you get up each morning and go to work, what inspires your lesson planning or keeps you going when you have a mountain of marking to do? Why do you teach?

Teaching and learning should always be about achieving the best outcomes for the learners. The learner experience, achievements and the impact our teaching has had on each individual learner should always be the driving force behind our teaching and assessment. As teachers and educators, our approaches to teaching and learning change over time. This is only natural. When training to teach there is a great deal of excitement, hours of creative lesson planning and resource making often goes into those all-important observations and we have a huge sense of purpose to make a change, to support learners and to change some of those policies, procedures or just areas of general practice we do not agree with. Then we start teaching. Suddenly, we are thrown into a world of constant marking, meetings and behaviour management. Not to mention the pastoral side of teaching that is all too often missed out of the teacher training curriculum. Throw into the mix a couple of bad lessons, which are inevitable, and you can often find yourself close to quitting.

There is no doubt about it that teaching is difficult. It is challenging, complicated and no two days or lessons will ever be the same. The preparation time required far exceeds the hours spent in the classroom and you will wake up in the middle of the night thinking of lesson ideas. So why do it? There are various reasons why individuals get involved in teaching. Some individuals have a false idea of what teaching is and fancy becoming a teacher for the holidays. Some people get involved in teaching because they want to make a difference. Some get involved because they are passionate about their subject and want to share it with others.

If you have become a teacher for the holidays then now is the time to hand in your resignation because you are most definitely in the wrong job. You will work through your holidays and your working day will never finish at 3pm. If your motivations for teaching are purely self-centred than it is not the job for you.

If you have become a teacher to make a difference or you have such a burning passion for your subject that you want to share it with others, excellent. Passion and education are where great change can begin. It is important to remember however that a simple desire for change or a love of a subject does not make teaching or bringing about change easy. It is very easy for both a desire to bring about change and a love of a subject to dwindle when teaching becomes tough, which it inevitably will do.

Regardless of individual reasons for getting into teaching, the true focus of teaching should always be achieving the best outcomes for the learners. To do this we need to not only understand our learners and how they learn, we also need to do something with that knowledge. Simply understanding it is not enough. We need to be willing to make changes. For many, change can be a scary thing, particularly if there are no guarantees that the changes will be one hundred percent effective. There are so many common phrases relating to changes, or rather a reluctance towards it. I am sure we have all heard the phrase 'if it's not broken don't fix it.'. This attitude is common amongst educators, particularly those that have been teachers for a long time and have long since found a rhythm to their teaching, one which they are reluctant to change because it works. The concept of something working is a complex one in the teaching world. What is the benchmark? How do we decide if something has 'worked?' If we are basing this on assessment results than I think the argument that current teaching practices are working can be effectively challenged.

Many of the changes that would be beneficial to adolescent learners, specifically those mentioned in this book, are scary to some teachers. They require effort, training and a sprinkle of faith. Without doubt it is easier to continue using the same schemes of work, lesson plans and resources year after year, it makes life easier for us. Having to adapt lessons year after year, week after week, takes time and we are already stretched for time. The cold, hard reality is that this is not good enough. Teaching is not about what is easiest for the teacher, it is not about the quickest way of getting things done and it is not about connivence. Teaching is about the best outcomes for the learners, it is about teaching them in a way that engages them, a way that allows them to take control of their own learning, that prepares them for their futures. It is not enough to do the basics because 'they work.' The horse and cart still work but they are not as effective as a car. Make your focus the learner experience, get to know your learners, make changes and keep learning.

References

Adriani, W and Laviola, G. (2004). Elevated levels of impulsivity and reduced pace conditioning with D-amphetamine: Two behavioural Features of Adolescence, Journal of Behavioural Neuroscience, (4), 695-703.

Andrews, J, Hutchinson, J and Johnes, R. (2016). Grammar Schools and Social Mobility, London: Education Policy Institute.

Bene, R and Dermarin, V. (2014). Neuroplasticity. PERIODICUM BIOLOGORUM UDC 57:61 VOL. 116, No 2, 209–211, 2014.

Blakemore,S-J .andMills,K.L.(2014) Is adolescence a sensitive period for sociocultural processing? Annu. Rev. Psychol. 65, 187–207.

Blakemore, S and Choudhury, S. (2006). Development of the adolescent brain: implications for executive function and social cognition, The Journal of Child Psychology and Psychiatry, 47 (3).

Blair, C and Raver, C. (2016). Poverty, Stress and Brain Development: New Directions for Prevention and Intervention, Academic Paediatrics.

Carlson, S, Easterday, M, Gerber, E and Lewis, D. (2018). Challenges of Peer Instruction in an Undergraduate Student-Led Learning Community Bi-Directional Diffusion as a Crucial Institutional Process, Instructional Science, 46 (3).

Casey, B. J., Jones, R. M., & Somerville, L. H (2011). Braking and accelerating the teen brain. Journal of Research on Adolescence, 21(1), 21-33. doi:10.1111/j.1532. 7795.2010.00712.x.

Casey, B, Jones, R and Hare, T. (2008). The Adolescent brain Annals of the New York Academy of Sciences, 1124, 111-126

Catharine R. Gale, Finbar J. O'Callaghan, Keith M. Godfrey, Catherine M. Law and Christopher N. Martyn Critical periods of brain growth and cognitive function in children Brain Advance Access published November 25, 2003.

Clapper, T. (2009). Moving Away From Teaching and Becoming a Facilitator of Learning, PAILAL 2 (2), 1-6.

Crone, E, Durston, S, Poldrack, R and Smith, S. (2010). The Role of Puberty in the Developing Adolescent Brain, Human Brain Mapping, University Medical Centre.

Crone, E and Dahl, R. (2012) Understanding adolescence as a period of social- affective engagement and goal flexibility, Nature reviews neuroscience, 13, 636-650.

Chandler, P and Sweller, J. (1991). Cognitive Load Theory and the Format of Instruction, Cognition and Instruction.

Department for Education (DfE) (2020). School Leaving Age, [online] available at https://www.gov.uk/know-when-you-can-leave-school Accessed 9th February 2020.

Ehlers, A, Hackmann, A and Michael, T. (2004). Intrusive Re-Experiencing in Post-Traumatic Stress Disorder: Phenomenology, Theory and Therapy, England, Hove.

Feinstein, S. (2004). Secrets of the Teenage Brain, CA, USA, The Brain Store.

Findlay, H. (2014). Technologies Transforming The Brain and Impacting Various Aspects of Societal Life, Journal of Healthcare, Science and Humanities, 2, 92-113.

Hair, N, Hanson, J, Wolfe, B and Pollak, S. (2015). Association of Child Poverty, Brain Development and Academic Achievement, JAMA Paediatrics.

Harden, R. M. and J. Crosby (2000). AMEE Guide No 20: The good teacher is more than a lecturer the twelve roles of the teacher. Medical Teacher 22(4), 334–347.

Hestenes, D. (1987). How The Brain Works: The Next Great Scientific Revolution, In Maximum Entropy and Bayesian Spectral Analysis and Estimation Problems, 173-205.

Howard-Jones, P. (2016). Neuroscience and Education: Issues and Opportunities, Teaching and Learning Research Programme, 1-27.

Kappen, P. (2007). Schools, Poverty and the Achievement Gap.

Kurchirko, Y. (2007). On differences and deficits: A critique of the theoretical and methodological underpinnings of the word gap, Journal of Early Childhood Literacy, New York.

Pastor, A. (2020). Memory Systems of the brain. Universitat Oberta de Catalunya, Computer Science, Multimedia and Telecommunications Department, Barcelona, Spain.

Pickering, S and Howard-Jones, P (2007). Educators' views on the role of neuroscience in education: A study of uk and international perspectives, mind, body and education, 1, 3.

Steinberg, L. (2008). A Social Neuroscience Perspective on Adolescent risk-taking, Developmental review, 28, 78-10.

Jade I'Anson-Milner

Jade I'Anson-Milner is an early years lecturer specialising in early years and the neuroscience of learning. She has an MA in Education and is currently completing her PhD.

Other books written by Jade I'Anson-Milner

Brain restarting Please wait….

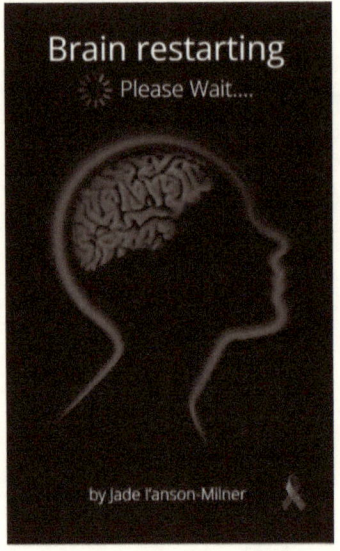

What is it like to live with a hidden disability? One that affects your life more than people know. You feel as though you're the only person going through it. Let me tell you, you're not. Living with Epilepsy has changed my life and not for the better. Am I alone? No..and neither are you. This book is not my life with epilepsy, but just a few things I've noticed along the way.

www.ingramcontent.com/pod-product-compliance
Lightning Source LLC
Chambersburg PA
CBHW021117080526
44587CB00010B/546